Guided Journal

This journal belongs to:

___

My intentions with this journal are:

___
___
___
___
___
___

Just Like The
Moon
We Go Through
Phases
But We Always Remain
Whole

Copyright | 2023 by Kendra Fierce

No part of this publication may be reproduced, stored in a retrieval system or transmitted in any form or by any means, electronic, mechanical, photocopying, recording, scanning, or otherwise, except as permitted under Section 13 of the Canadian Copyright Act, without the prior written permission of the Publisher. Requests to the Publisher for permission should be addressed to Kendra Fierce PO Box 80019 Airdrie, AB T4B 2V5.

Limit of Liability/Disclaimer of Warranty: The publisher and the author make no representations or warranties with respect to the accuracy or completeness of the contents of this work and specifically disclaim all warranties, including without limitation warranties of fitness for a particular purpose. No warranty may be created or extended by sales or promotional materials. The advice and strategies contained herein may not be suitable for every situation. This work is sold with the understanding that the publisher and author are not engaged in rendering medical, legal, or other professional advice or services. If professional assistance is required, the services of a competent professional should be sought. Neither the Publisher nor the author shall be liable for damages arising here from. The fact that an individual, organization, or website may be referred to in this work as a citation and/or potential source of information does not mean the author or the publisher endorses all of the information the individual, organization or website may provide or recommendations they may make. Further, the readers should be aware that any internet websites listed in this work may have changed or disappeared between when the work was written and when it is read.

Written & Designed by | Kendra Fierce

Table of Contents

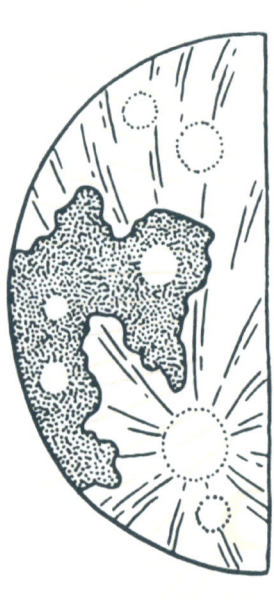

3	Copyright
4	Table Of Contents
6	Introduction
7	The Phases
10	New Moon
11	Waxing Crescent
12	First Quarter
13	Waxing Gibbous
14	Full Moon
15	Waning Gibbous
16	Last Quarter
17	Waning Crescent
18	And it Continues
19	Moon Events
20	Supermoons
21	Lunar Eclipses
22	Eclipse Phases
23	Dark/Black Moons
24	Red/White Moon Cycle
25	Moon Rituals
26	New Moon Manifestation Ritual
41	Full Moon Release Ritual
55	The Zodiacs
59	The Houses
60	The Journal

Introduction

Like the phases of the moon, we transition many times as we journey through life. Each phase brings different energy, trials, tribulations, as well as opportunities to learn and grow.

The beginning of this Guided Journal will explain the astronomy of the 8 moon cycles as well as some basic astrology. Then it will express in great detail Kendra's New Moon Manifestation Ritual as well as her Full Moon Release Ritual which will help you take full advantage of all of this incredible energy.

Astronomy is the branch of science that deals with celestial objects, space, and the physical universe as a whole.

Astrology is the study of the movements and relative positions of celestial bodies interpreted as having an influence on human affairs and the natural world.

Keep in mind this journal was written with the hopes that no matter your experience and/or background you will feel comfortable going through the steps. The rituals were designed to help you reach your goals easier using a mixture of purposeful journaling, cognitive behavioural therapy, and self-reflection. Feel free to add or omit anything that you feel will assist you through the manifestation, shadow work, and healing process.

The Phases

The moon goes through 8 phases as it travels through its orbit around the Earth every 29.5 days. This is also known as the lunar month.

You will notice that generally New and Full moons do not fall on the same day every month and that is because the Gregorian calendar months regularly used do not reflect the lunar month and are not an equal number of days per month. For the most part, you can count on having one full cycle per month however in some cases you may experience multiple new or full moons in the same calendar month. These are also known as Dark or Black Moons. There is more about those on page 23.

As the moon travels through its phases the energy may be transformative or stressful depending on many factors but most importantly how this energy affects your life will depend on your mindset. It is your personal choice whether or not you perform rituals. It's also up to you how and when you perform them.

FUN FACT: no matter where you live on the planet the moon is always in the same phase for everyone.

New Moon
Manifestation & New Beginnings

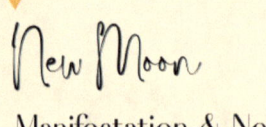

Waxing Crescent
Inspired Action and Momentum

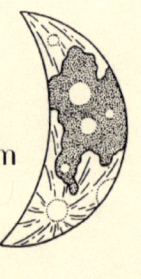

First Quarter
Strength & Perseverance

Waxing Gibbous
Hard Work & Development

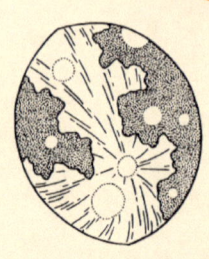

New Moon

ASTRONOMY

A New Moon happens when the Sun, Moon and, Earth are on the same ecliptic longitude. The Moon reflects the light back to the sun therefore the lunar disc is not visible to us on Earth which means there is no moonlight during a new moon.

ASTROLOGY

A New Moon brings exciting energy that is all about new beginnings and manifestation. It is a great time to work on your goals and step into new chapters of your life. Use this inspired energy to clean up your space and purge items that no longer serve you to make room for your manifestations to flow in. Partake in anything that helps raise your vibration such as adventuring in nature and exploring your creative side. Listen to music, enjoy time with your friends and family, eat healthy food, drink lots of water, and remember to practice gratitude daily. This is also a great time to perform a New Moon Manifestation Ritual. There is one included in this journal on page 26.

Waxing Creesent

ASTRONOMY

This phase occurs between the New Moon and the First Quarter. The moon is starting to become illuminated again. The Moon travels through the Waxing Crescent phase for 6.375 days.

ASTROLOGY

The energy of the Waxing Crescent is inspired action. This is the next step towards your goals and the things you manifested during the New Moon. Opportunities will now be presenting themselves to you. If you are open to them of course! So ensure you are maintaining your high vibration and most importantly practicing gratitude daily. Staying present in the moment will bring you more peace and it will make it easier for you to spot new opportunities as soon as they are presented to you. Then the question becomes, "Does this align with my higher self, yes or no?" Make the most of what comes your way and the challenges you take on now will lead to monumental growth.

First Quarter

ASTRONOMY

At this point the Moon has travelled a quarter of the way through its orbit. It's a confusing title however because half of the moon is visible to us on Earth. On the Northern Hemisphere the right side of the moon is illuminated and on the Southern Hemisphere it's the left.

ASTROLOGY

The energy of the First Quarter is strength and perseverance. The moon is now in the "Yang" phase of its cycle. It's time to keep pushing forward towards your goals and manifestations. At this point, you may have experienced some bumps in the road so this is also a good time to do a quick re-evaluation and check in with your higher self to make sure you are in alignment. If you are still on the preferred path remember that these bumps are there to teach you lessons, test your courage, and give you opportunities for growth so you can increase your vibration to what's needed for those goals. Make sure you are staying action oriented. There is time to rest in future phases.

Waxing Gibbous

ASTRONOMY

The moon is now heading towards becoming completely illuminated. The Moon travels through the Waxing Gibbous phase for 6.375 days.

ASTROLOGY

The energy of the Waxing Gibbous is hard work and development. As you journey towards your manifestations, it is important to remember you will never have complete control over the outcome but you do have control over your mindset when you get there. As the Moon heads into its Full Moon phase, the Waxing Gibbous gives you time to focus on staying in the flow and releasing any need for control as you continue your forward momentum. You may be tested even more during this phase and as emotions start to surface ensure you are taking note of them so you can fully release them during the Full Moon. Practicing daily gratitude is one of THE BEST ways to stay present in the moment and keep an abundant mindset. Keeping your vibrations high during this phase is also really important.

Full Moon

ASTRONOMY

A Full Moon happens when the Sun, Earth, and Moon are in the same ecliptic longitude and the moon is reflecting the sun's light back to the Earth. The Moon is now fully illuminated and though it appears this way for about 3 days it's only actually full for a brief moment.

ASTROLOGY

Full Moon energy can be extremely heavy but also transformative. This is the time to release what no longer serves you and as well as anything that could be holding you back from your manifestations. You can do this through journalling as well as the Full Moon release ritual in this journal on page 41. Statistically, there are also more people in the emergency rooms so it is imperative to take note of the emotions you are feeling and find healthy ways to release them. This is the time for healing and guidance. Self-care during this time is also key to ensuring you stay on top of everything that may be surfacing. This is also a great time to purge items you no longer need as well as release (with love) relationships that feel draining and/or don't allow you to be yourself.

Waning Gibbous

ASTRONOMY

The illumination of the moon is now shrinking from 99.1 to 50.1%. The word gibbous refers to the oval/round shape that the moon now appears to us on Earth. The Moon travels through the Waning Gibbous phase for 6.375 days.

ASTROLOGY

The energy of the Waning Gibbous is healing and communication. Instead of focusing outwards like the energy of the Waxing Gibbous, it's time to focus inwards. Working on shadow work during this time is HIGHLY recommended. Shadow work is the process of acknowledging and healing the limiting thoughts and behaviour patterns that could be preventing you from fully aligning with your higher self. During this time progress might feel slower than anticipated but keep in mind the work that you do now is actually what puts your manifestations into overdrive. This is also a great time to set and communicate boundaries with the people in your life. Ensuring you are keeping up with your self-care routine is also important to stay grounded as the emotions from the Full Moon may still be lingering.

Last Quarter

ASTRONOMY

Also known as the Third Quarter the Moon is now half-illuminated once more. The Moon has now travelled 3/4 of the way through its orbit. Just like the Full and New moon this phase only lasts a brief moment.

ASTROLOGY

The energy of the Last Quarter is release, transition and responsibility. Taking control of your mindset through Shadow Work and other healing modalities will allow you to move into new chapters and phases of your life a little bit easier. Releasing the energies that no longer serve you will increase your vibration and give you space to bring in your manifestations. As you heal, grow, and work towards your manifestations your vibration changes so use this time to take a look at the important areas of your life to see how the energies are aligning with your new vibration. Then it's time to decide what you need to let go of in order to continue your journey. This is where you will start noticing full or partial shifts in your progress.

Waning Crescent

ASTRONOMY

This is the last phase before we reach the New Moon once more. This Moon travels through this phase for 6.375 days while only a small sliver of the moon is illuminated and visible to us on Earth.

ASTROLOGY

The energy of the Waning Crescent is contemplation, celebration, and personal growth. The Last Quarter and the Waning Gibbous phase were about healing and releasing what no longer serves you while the Waning Crescent phase is about acknowledging yourself as a whole so you can fine-tune your habits and structures. Part of healing is celebrating how far you have come and everything you have accomplished thus far. This is the perfect time to do so. You may still feel like the energy is moving slowly but remember this is a sign that it's time for reflection and self-care. Take a break to treat yourself before you head into the forward momentum of the New Moon phase once again.

And it Continues

After the Waning Crescent phase, the lunar disc once again becomes invisible to us on Earth as we experience another New Moon.

THE FULL LUNAR CYCLE

New Moon
Waxing Gibbous
First Quarter
Waxing Crescent
Full Moon
Waning Gibbous
Last Quarter
Waning Crescent

Moon Events

As the Moon travels through its phases we on Earth experience some pretty cool Moon events and they can also bring some pretty intense energy! Similar to the energy of the Full Moon, the energy of the other phases of the Moon with the addition of Sun events, can be both stressful and transformative. If you are prepared and are taking care of your body, mind, and soul these events should be something to look forward to not only scientifically but spiritually. It can be an amazing time for growth and expansion through personal introspection.

Keep in mind spiritually and culturally Moon events have many meanings around the world. With this fact in mind, this journal will be explaining some of the events scientifically and then giving you some basic spiritual recommendations.

As always feel free to add or omit anything the works with your own personal beliefs and practices.

Supermoons

ASTRONOMY

Also known as perigean Full Moon by astronomers, a Supermoon happens when the Moons orbit is at its closest point to the earth. You most likely will not be able to see a difference without a telescope but in some cases the Moon may appear bigger and/or brighter. A Supermoon can happen during a New or Full Moon.

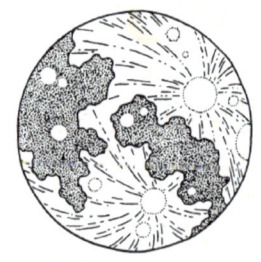

ASTROLOGY

Supermoons can intensify the energy of the particular lunar phase the Moon is in. It is important to practice self-care and go with your flow when deciding if you are up for the New Moon Manifestation Ritual or a Full Moon Release Ritual.

Each Supermoon will happen in a specific zodiac sign. This sign can dictate the energy surrounding the Supermoon and can help give you clarity surrounding emotions being brought up at this time. There is a basic breakdown of the energy of each sign on page 55 of this journal.

Lunar Eclipses

ASTRONOMY

A lunar eclipse happens when the Earth blocks the Suns light that would otherwise reflect off of the Moon. A lunar eclipse can only occur at a Full Moon and there are three different types. Total, partial, and penumbral.

ASTROLOGY

A lunar eclipse has many meanings spiritually around the world. Some cultures believe it is bad luck to be out during a lunar eclipse and some believe they are a cosmic reset. No matter what you believe they can definitely be a time of deep transformation. Considering a lunar eclipse can only happen during a Full Moon, taking this time to work on releasing emotional blocks and cleansing your space is recommended. They are thought to bring on abrupt and unexpected change which can be stressful if you are not prepared. Ensure you are taking care of yourself and release expectations of the outcome. Have faith in flow and enjoy the ride!

Eclipse Phases

TOTAL LUNAR ECLIPSE

A total lunar eclipse happens when the Sun, Earth, and the Moon are perfectly aligned and Earths shadow completely covers the moon. During its maximum eclipse point the lunar disc is still visible to the eye but it will cast a dim glow that can sometimes appear red which is called a "blood moon". While the eclipse is happening, if you are unaware of the event it may just appear like the moon is in different phases because the shadow is dark until full coverage.

PARTIAL LUNAR ECLIPSE

A partial lunar eclipse is similar to the total eclipse however the Sun, Earth, and the Moon are not directly aligned and only a portion of the Moon is covered by the Earths shadow. What we see on Earth depends on how everything is lined up.

PENUMBRAL LUNAR ECLIPSE

A penumbral eclipse is when the Moon is in the Earths faint penumbral shadow. On Earth this eclipse is won't be noticed unless you are a seasoned sky watcher

Dark/Black Moons

ASTRONOMY

A Dark or Black Moon happens when there are more or fewer New or Full Moons in a single calendar month than normal. The most commonly used Gregorian calendar months do not align with the lunar calendar which has an equal 29.5 days per month. Due to this, depending on which calendar you follow, you may experience dark/black Moons. A huge thing to note is that the lunar phases do not actually change. So if you are in the habit of preparing your goals during the New Moon and releasing limiting thoughts and emotions during the Full Moon it is best to maintain this schedule.

ASTROLOGY

Dark or Black Moons have many different meanings spiritually. My best suggestion is to take note of the emotions you are feeling at the time and act accordingly.

If you are feeling a lot of heavy emotions take some time for self-care and perform the Full Moon Release Ritual. If you are feeling motivated and inspired, strike while the iron is hot and perform the New Moon Manifestation Ritual. Whatever you choose remember to Be You, Do You, For You!

White/Red Moon Cycle

Do you menstruate or get your period on or close to the New or Full Moon? In a lot of cultures and practices, this has some significance. It is said, if you are aligned with the New Moon you are on the **White Moon Cycle** and if you sync up with the Full Moon you are on the **Red Moon Cycle**.

There are different meanings for each depending on what you practice but I can guarantee that if you are on either cycle your **INTUITION IS ON POINT** especially during this time and you should take advantage of the potential growth opportunities.

If you are on the **White Moon Cycle** take time to focus your energy inwards. This is a more nurturing cycle and focusing on self-care during this time is recommended. The energy is reflection, healing, and introspection. You most likely spend a lot of time helping others so use this time to fill back up your cup. It can also indicate more maternal energy.

If you are on the **Red Moon Cycle** this is a passionate and forward-thinking energy. During this time empower yourself and others around you.

If you **switch between cycles** take note of the energies during your menstrual cycle and act accordingly. If you are not synced with either that is ok too! The middle cycles are sometimes known as the **Pink and Purple Cycles** which have transitional but still progressive energy.

Moon Rituals

Performing New and Full Moon rituals are an amazing way to honour the moon and her phases as well as yourself. Any rituals and spirituality aside it is also a great way to set and keep track of your goals, personal and professionally.

It's for this reason that I personally suggest you do not skip out on rituals during Dark/Black Moons. There could be many in one year depending on your definition so it could really affect your ability to stay consistent. The main focus of this journal and these rituals is to help you create a sustainable, healthy schedule that allows you to find your flow and travel through life with as much ease as possible.

The following rituals use the concepts of cognitive behavioural therapy and purposeful journaling. As mentioned in previous chapters, these rituals have been left open to allow anyone of any age, with any background to participate. That being said, if you have other tools and things you would like to add feel free to integrate them into your practice with this journal.

There is no specific time or way you need to perform my Full and New Moon rituals. If you are in the mood to set goals do the New Moon Manifestation Ritual and if you are feeling some heavy emotions do the Full Moon Release Ritual.

New Moon Manifestation Ritual

New Moons are generally about new beginnings, high vibrations, and manifestation. Manifestation is bringing to fruition any goal or desire and it can be done in a variety of ways. No matter what method you choose, the most important thing while you manifest is always how you **FEEL**. During a New Moon while you work on your goals you can ask yourself, what would you like to manifest in the next 30 days? Or before the next New Moon? Some goals you will be able to accomplish right away however some goals may take "many moons" to complete. It is recommended to make long-term goals however it's the smaller goals that really help you make progress towards your larger ones.

This ritual is designed to help you connect with your higher self to create and achieve fulfilling, meaningful goals. Using the concepts of cognitive behavioural therapy mixed with purposeful journaling, this manifestation ritual will not only help you create amazing goals but it will help you find more calm and purpose in your life.

There are 11 steps to this ritual but as mentioned in the previous chapter, feel free to add or omit anything you would like.

How long it will take to complete this ritual will depend on how you experience each individual step. My only recommendation is to find a comfortable space and take your time. The steps will be outlined in detail in the upcoming chapters.

Materials Required

The basic materials required to complete this New Moon Manifestation Ritual are as follows.
Keep in mind you are more than welcome to add or omit anything to keep it aligned with your personal values and abilities.

YOU WILL NEED:

This journal or pieces of paper and a pen/pencil

Anything you need for your sacred space

OPTIONALLY

Music

Bay Leaves or Small Pieces of Paper

A Felt Tip Pen

Fire Safe Bowl

Lighter

STEP ONE

Cleanse & Clear

Cleansing and clearing your space is a completely individual practice so this section will be left open for interpretation. The key thing to remember is a clear space is a clear mind. Having this clarity will allow you to better picture your goals and manifestations.

Before you begin your ritual taking some time to tidy your space is beneficial for a few reasons and the fact that it feels good to complete these tasks is actually chemical.

The brain releases the reward chemicals serotonin and dopamine as you complete tasks and even when you are just thinking about completing them. This increases your vibration and makes you feel awesome!

Manifestation is best done when you are feeling great and your vibes are high so starting off by cleansing and clearing your space not only makes you feel good but sets the intention for the rest of the ritual.

If there are other cleansing practices feel free to incorporate them into this ritual.
The last step in the ritual is a New Moon Cleansing Bath or Shower so feel free to add these practices to the end as well.

STEP TWO

Create Your Sacred Space

Creating a sacred space for yourself to complete these rituals not only helps you solidify a routine but it sets good intentions for the practice. This space does not have to be anything more than a comfortable space with the tools you require for your rituals. However, feel free to jazz it up with anything that increases your vibration and makes you feel connected to your higher self.

ITEMS YOU CAN ADD TO YOUR SACRAD SPACE

Crystals
Insense
Music
Blankets
Candles
Visual Art
Talismans
Prayer Beads/Books
Singing Bowls
Pillows
Essential Oils and Diffusers

STEP THREE

Music gives a soul to the universe, wings to the mind, flight to the imagination, and life to everything – Plato.

Everything on this planet has a vibration and music is one of the most easily accessible tools we have to change our mood and vibration almost instantaneously. Using music to double down on your manifestation results is highly recommended! You are more than welcome to choose any kind of music you would like however binaural beats create auditory illusions to adjust your vibration quickly and sometimes quite significantly.

A binaural beat is created when you hear two tones, one in each ear, that are slightly different in frequency. Your brain processes a third beat at the difference of the frequencies.

For example: if one ear is hearing 130hz and one is hearing 120hz your brain will hear 10hz in ADDITION to the original tones.
They are used to tune instruments and most recently have been connected to potential health benefits.

If you are looking for them you can search "Binaural Beats for Manifestation" on most streaming applications. They have binaural beats for pretty much anything you can think of!

It doesn't really matter what music you choose it is always about how it makes you FEEL! The energy of manifestation is limitless and inspiring. Your music should help you feel the same.

STEP FOUR

Meditation & Visualization

If you are new to meditation it isn't necessarily about clearing your mind. In my opinion, as humans in the society we live in this is almost impossible. I like to think of it more like check-in and alignment.

Who is "driving the bus" right now? Who is in control of your automatic thoughts?
Has your inner critic been giving you a hard time?
Is your shadow self in "protection mode" and preventing you from moving forward?
Are you in alignment with your higher self?
Or are you just on autopilot?

Then comes the alignment. Where would you like to be and how would you like to feel?
Close your eyes, place one hand on your chest and one hand on your stomach and breath deeply. Imagine you are living YOUR BEST LIFE! Imagine every little detail. Also focus on the energy you would like to bring with you throughout this ritual.

This visualization process releases dopamine and serotonin in your brain which are feel-good, reward chemicals. This builds anticipation and positive feelings in your body which improve your mindset and increases your vibration.

STEP FIVE
Gratitude

No matter what phase the moon is in and no matter where you are in life one thing to note is the impermanence of it all.

You, as you know it is a temporary fixture on this planet and until your physical energy is returned to the Earth and your soul heads on its next journey (if that's something you believe) one of the best things you can do is express gratitude daily for all of the abundance available to you in the present.

If you are working on creating a more positive mindset this is one of the easiest, most effective ways to begin. Practicing daily gratitude releases dopamine and serotonin in your brain which will help you create more positive neural pathways. Over time this will lead to more positive automatic responses.

It's very simple. During this ritual and every day, write down 11 or more things you are grateful for in the present. Try to remove the ownership. Meaning removing the word "my". We do not own anything on this planet. Everything is temporary because we are temporary. Instead, look at the things and people in your life for the qualities they possess and what is amazing about them. This allows you to see things as they are on the planet, not just as they are to you.

For example, instead of saying "my house" you can be grateful for a beautiful home. Instead of "my family" you can be grateful for a supportive family that cares a lot about each other and loves having fun.

STEP SIX

Higher Self Connection

Your higher self is, in essence, an extension of you. Just like we have our shadow self as our protector on the flip side we have our higher self as our guide. How do you want to **FEEL** as you journey through life? We don't have control over outside circumstances. We only have control over our mindset when we get there. That goes for other peoples feelings and choices as well. We can only control how we respond to them.

Connecting with your higher self is something you should do often and it is something that will evolve over time. As you start aligning with the energy of your higher self decisions in life become **A LOT** easier.
Does this align with my higher self yes or no?

So how do you connect with your higher self?
It starts with determining the traits and qualities of your higher self. I call this "BOSS MODE ACTIVATED" so don't hold back! For example, my higher self is calm, non-reactive, emotional and financially independently secure, consistent, courageous, and a guide to name a few. **Do not hold yourself back here!** Remember your thoughts align your emotion which aligns your actions so if you can think it you can attain it.

Start with "My Higher Self Is" or "I Am" then list as many as you can think of. Once complete, read the list out loud and visualize the energy of your higher self. If you are struggling, add "What If" in front of each one. IE: What if I am consistent? It's human nature to answer and this will help you feel the energy of aligning with your higher self traits easier.

STEP SEVEN

Manifestation Letter

Now that you have completed your setup, check-in, alignment, and you are in "Manifestation Mode" let's write a letter to solidify this amazing energy. This letter not only helps you identify your goals and manifestations but it is useful down the road for shadow work and to continue working on your manifestations.
If writing the letter is too much feel free to use voice notes but try to get it out of your head if you can.

Start with Dear, My Higher Self, Universe, Spirit, God, or whatever you prefer.
Then describe where you are in life right now and how that makes you feel. No matter what emotions you are feeling. Do not hold yourself back here and be honest. This release not only feels good but it helps you make space for new energy. It also helps you acknowledge limiting thoughts and behaviours that could be holding you back from aligning with your higher self and receiving your manifestations.
Next, express what you would like to manifest and how that makes you feel. Remember to keep it in the present tense and be descriptive if you can but not restrictive. **BIG DIFFERENCE!**

For example, I feel relieved and excited to be financially stable as a full-time author and artist in a field that I love. (that's mine)
Don't hold yourself back here either! You are more than capable of accomplishing mostly anything. You do not have to worry about how it works out you just need to work and it will work out.
Finally, express gratitude for your opportunities, abundances, and anything else you would like.
Then sign it with the name, sign, or symbol that you resonate with the most.

STEP SEVEN CONTINUED

It is up to you what you would like to do with the letter however I recommend that you save it for a couple of reasons.

This letter not only includes your manifestations but as mentioned it has future uses. For approximately two weeks after the New Moon, the energy has forward momentum. The paths to your manifestations will start to appear as soon as you even **THINK** about them. Writing them down and other manifestation techniques just help remind you of the energy of your manifestations. They are tools to help you get there.
You need to put inspired action behind your inspired energy by taking steps every day to get to your goals. You need to make choices, head down the paths, overcome obstacles, and raise your vibration to get to your manifestations.

During the Full Moon, you can take out this list, check in with what you were manifesting, and if you don't have what you were looking for what do you need to release to get there?
You can perform my Full Moon Release Ritual to help you out which is located on page 41.

It is also good to keep as a reminder of the energy you were experiencing at this time. You are able to use it for visualization or just as a reminder of how far you've come.

If you really want to burn it... make two copies!

All of that aside, with everything going on in life and in our brains it is near impossible to remember everything we wrote which would make it tricky to take consistent daily actions towards your goals.

As always, go with your own flow but as you can see there are many effective reasons to save it.

STEP EIGHT
Manifestation Prompts

If you would like to deepen your manifestation and journaling practice you can work with prompts. Journal prompts are statements and/or questions that deepen your thought process about various subjects.

There are many places to find them including Pinterest and Google however I have included a list of my favorite manifestation prompts below:

- What does a dream day in your life look and feel like?
- What is your definition of abundance?
- How do you want to feel when you first wake up in the morning? Do you feel that way now? If not, what changes can you make in your life to get you there?
- What activities bring you the most joy and why? Can you bring more of this into your life?
- Express in detail your dream vacation?
- What is one thing you have always wanted to learn more about? And how can you start going about
- How do you want people to feel when they are around you?
- When do you feel the most confident and aligned with your higher self? And how can you add more of that to your current schedule?
- What are your favourite parts of yourself (not just physically) and why?
- What is your definition of success?
- What is one important manifestation you are working on and why is it important to you?

STEP NINE – OPTIONAL

Bay Leaf Manifestation

There are many methods and many cultures that use bay leaves for manifestation. Bay leaves are natural and have a naturally high vibration however most paper we use today is full of chemicals and is created from destroying the tree completely.

If you do not have access to bay leaves it is more than fine to use paper. Remember manifestation is about aligning the thought, which aligns the emotion which aligns the actions. BOOM Manifestation! Go with your flow and use what you have available to you.

WHAT YOU'LL NEED

Dried Bay Leaves or Small Pieces of Paper
Felt tip pen (anything will write on paper but felt tip is required for the bay leaves)
Scissor or Tweezers
Fire Safe Bowl
Lighter
Water (just in case)

Step 1 | close your eyes and focus on the amazing energy you have cultivated during this ritual

Step 2 | choose the manifestations that you would like to give extra energy to and write them on the bay leaves or the small pieces of paper

Step 3 | hold them individually in the scissors or tweezers (THIS IS VERY IMPORTANT – THEY BURN VERY UNEXPECTEDLY) and read them out loud boldly before you light them on fire

It is said if they burn quickly your manifestations are coming sooner than you think. If it's a slow or incomplete burn you may have some extra shadow work you need to complete to get there but it's still possible.

STEP TEN

New Moon Bath or Shower

The New Moon bath or shower is a mandatory activity to celebrate everything you have overcome to bring you to this moment. It is self-care to celebrate your strength and courage.

For many reasons we are very conditioned to always be on the lookout for ways to change, evolve, or have a different energy than we do right in this moment. Thinking about the past or thinking about the future constantly prevents us from enjoying the present moment and appreciating ourselves just we are.

Thinking about the future can bring on feelings of anxiety and thinking about the past can make us feel sad and/or depressed.
If you are struggling to "**find happiness**" this is just a reminder that if you are looking for happiness in people, places, or things you are in the pursuit of happiness and that can be indefinite. Your brain releases serotonin and dopamine when you "chase" your happiness and when you reach your goals you most likely will not be satisfied for long. Your brain will want that stimulation again which means you may also find yourself self-sabotaging so you can chase a new relationship or new career etc.
Happiness is a choice. At some point you need to decide you ARE a happy person and you will make choices that align with that daily because that's what you deserve.

If you struggle with that, remember you can be a happy person working on your anxiety. You can be a happy person with a mental illness. You can be a happy person having a bad day. You can be more than one thing at a time.

STEP ELEVEN

High Vibe Activities

As mentioned, there are many tools and ways you can manifest however the most important thing is always how you feel while doing it. With this in mind, it is important to not only keep your vibrations high during this ritual but continue to increase them over the next 2 weeks as you head down the paths towards your manifestations. Choose a few high vibe activities to complete over the next two weeks before the Full Moon.

Completing high vibration activities releases dopamine and serotonin in your brain which are motivation and reward chemicals. Therefore the continual production of them will help you overcome any obstacles that present themselves. This leads to higher success rates in your manifestations.

HIGH VIBE ACTIVITIES INCLUDE

Practicing Daily Gratitude
Exploring Nature
Exercise
Drinking 3-4L of Water per Day
Reading
Meditation
Visualization
Yoga
Sound Baths
Working with Spiritual Tools such as Crystals/Tarot
Nourish Your Body with Nutritious Food
Serving Your Community
Tidying Up Your Personal Space

Your High Vibe Activities

Make a list of the activities that raise your vibration and bring you joy! Try to align them with your higher self.

Full Moon Release Ritual

Full Moon energy can be super intense! Statistically, there are even more people in the emergency rooms. You may also notice children can also be very sensitive to this energy. When you have control over you mindset these challenges becomes chances for change!

During the New Moon and the time following you worked on your manifestations and connecting with your higher self.
It's now time to ask yourself, have I received my manifestations? If not there could be limiting thoughts and behaviour patterns that you may hold that could be preventing you from fully aligning with the vibration of what you want.
Full Moon energy is about releasing what no longer serves you so this is a perfect time to work on releasing these limitations as well.

When we decide to manifest, the paths open up however it is up to us to walk down them, overcome the obstacles, raise our vibration to meet the vibration of our manifestations, and achieve our goals. If this is not happing it could be for a few reasons but most of the time it comes down to a lack of confidence. We are usually the only ones holding ourselves back from truly discovering all that we can accomplish.
The following Full Moon Release Ritual is designed to help you connect with your higher self and shadow self through cognitive behaviour therapy and purposeful journalling to locate and release limiting thoughts and patterns.

Materials Required

The basic materials required to complete this Full Moon Release Ritual are as follows:

Keep in mind you are more than welcome to add or omit anything to keep it aligned with your personal values and abilities.

YOU WILL NEED:

This journal or pieces of paper and a pen/pencil

Anything you need for your sacred space

<u>OPTIONALLY</u>

Music

Small Pieces of Paper

A Pen/Pencil

Fire Safe Bowl

Lighter

Water for safety

STEP ONE
Cleanse & Clear

We talked about cleansing and clearing your space in the New Moon Manifestation Ritual and this is a similar process. Full Moon energy is about releasing what no longer serves you so this is a great time to tidy your space and release with gratitude items you no longer use.

You will still be releasing serotonin and dopamine as you complete tasks so this will help combat anxious emotions you may feel parting with belongings. They also keep you motivated to progress through bigger tasks.

OTHER FULL MOON CLEANSING IDEAS

Clean out your dresser, purge items, refold
Organize your "Junk Drawer"
Donate books you no longer read
Clean out your closet, purge items, and reorganize
Scrub your shower/tub
Organize under your sinks
Wash AND FOLD all of your laundry
Wash makeup sponges

STEP TWO

Create Your Sacrad Space

Full Moon release rituals can be emotional so it is imperative you are in a safe comfortable space where you can express yourself freely. This space does not have to be anything more than a comfortable space with the tools you require for your rituals. However, as mentioned feel free to jazz it up with anything that increases your vibration and makes you feel connected to your higher self.

PLACES TO FIND A SACRAD SPACE

Bedroom
Meditation Area
Sun Porch
Park
In Your Car
With Friends in a Designated Place
In a Private Break Room
Hotel/Motel Room

STEP THREE

Binaural Beats

Music taste is extremely personal so this is just a reminder that it is not so important what you listen to but how it makes you FEEL while you are listening to it. If you are struggling with what to choose, think about the energy you want to take with you throughout this Full Moon Release Ritual and search that word followed by binaural beats. You can do this through Google or YouTube.

Binaural beats between 1-30 Hz can induce the same states achieved in deep meditation. To potentially improve your meditation practice, throw on some headphones and explore how you feel listening to this music phenomenon.

Some other health benefits of Binaural Beats include

reduced anxiety
increased focus
increased relaxation
promotes creativity
pain management
improved memory and concentration

You can also choose specific beats depending on your desired state of mind:

- 1-4 HZ – Delta – Sleep & Relaxation
- 4-8 Hz – Theta – REM Sleep, reduced anxiety, relaxation, meditation, and creative states
- 8-13 Hz – Alpha – promotes positive feelings, decreased anxiety
- 14-30 Hz – Beta – increased concentration and alertness, problem-solving, and improved memory
- 40 Hz – enhanced training and learning

STEP FOUR

Meditation & Visualization

It's time for another check-in and alignment. Who is driving the bus right now? Is it your inner critic? Is your shadow self in protection mode? Are you feeling in alignment with your higher self?

Next, visualize how you want to feel as you go through this ritual. Focus on how much inner strength and power it takes to look inside yourself and choose to heal over hurt. The work you do today is making space for new energy to come into your life. Releasing what no longer serves you increases your capacity for new goals and it brings in your manifestations way sooner.

If you have been having trouble receiving your manifestations there are most likely limiting thoughts and behaviour patterns holding you back from fully aligning with the energy of those manifestations. While you are meditating and visualizing it's always good to imagine how it FEELS when you receive your manifestations. What does a day in the life of fully aligned YOU look like? Where are you living? Where are you vacationing? Visualize every little detail. More is definitely better. This helps solidify these vibrations into your subconscious which helps you make decisions on a daily basis that align with that.

STEP FIVE

Higher Self Connection

Just like you did during the New Moon Manifestation Ritual, connect with your higher self by listing the traits and qualities. I mentioned that this will evolve over time and you may find it evolving sooner than you think that's why it's a good idea to do it during the New Moon and the Full Moon. This will also give you a good idea of where your head is at during these times and how these energies might affect you going forward.

Upon further review, you may find that you are more emotional during the New Moon and you feel more high vibe during the Full Moon. If that is the case feel free to switch up the rituals to suit your energy.

Try to practice getting in touch with your higher self either by journaling or visualization before making decisions. You can simplify by asking yourself, does this align with my higher self, yes or no? Or you can just step into "Boss Mode" to bring you more confidence.

Remember, your higher self is your guide. There to assist you as you journey down the paths to your manifestations and there to support you while you work through your limiting thoughts. Turn to your higher self for inspiration and motivation. Even thinking about your higher self releases dopamine and serotonin which will help motivate you to continue to push towards your goals and create your dream life!

STEP SIX

Shadow Self Connection

Connecting with your higher self allows you to connect with your Shadow Self a little easier. Just like you have your Higher Self as your guide you have your shadow self as your protector. However over time, depending on your history, childhood, and traumas your Shadow Self has come up with behaviour patterns to protect you that may not be serving you in the present tense. I call this "PROTECTION MODE".

When your Shadow Self is in "protection mode" you may experience limiting thoughts and behaviours that could be preventing you from fully aligning with the energy of your Higher Self consistently and confidently.

Take a look at the list you created for your Higher Self then connect with your Shadow Self by listing its traits and qualities starting with "My Shadow Self Is...". It is the opposite of your Higher Self. Look at the traits of your Higher Self and ask yourself if you FEEL those qualities. If the answer is no then that would be a quality of your Shadow Self.
For example: if your Higher Self is confident and that's something you are struggling with, your Shadow Self is insecure.

It is important to look at this list with a solution-based mindset. Remind yourself that nobody is perfect and we all have shadows to work on. The fact that you are taking the time to acknowledge them and release their control over your life shows how incredibly STRONG you are!

STEP SEVEN

Letter of Foregiveness

You don't owe the person you were in the past anything other than gratitude for getting you to this point today and you don't deserve to carry around the baggage of others. You expressed your manifestations in a letter during the New Moon Manifestation Ritual so now it is time to dive deep and start releasing your attachment to old energy and situations to make space for new energy to come in.

Holding onto negative emotions from the past, especially against another person is like drinking poison and expecting the other person to die. It only hurts you and most times they won't even know you're upset. We have no control over anything/anyone else but we do have control over our mindsets when it comes to these situations. We may never receive apologies from people we may deserve them from so forgiveness in this sense isn'y saying "what happened is ok", it means you are saying "I am no longer carrying your baggage" and "I am no longer giving your energy to the situation positive or negative".

It doesn't matter who you address it to and the format is not important. You can start by explaining a situation you would like to release and how it made you feel. You can then express how it will feel to release this situation. You can finish with, "I now release my energy from this situation for my greater good and healing". This will help you create stronger, healthier boundaries and new neural pathways which will lead to healthier responses over time.

This letter is also extremely helpful for your shadow work sessions.
You also want to forgive yourself. Using the same format it's time to let yourself off the hook. If beating yourself was going to work, it would have worked by now. Explain the situation, how it made you feel, and how you will do it differently next time. This allows you to remain solution based. Everything you've done in your life has brought you up to this point and that's something worth celebrating!

STEP EIGHT

Release The Energy

It is not logical to look at either your Higher Self or your Shadow Self and expect to achieve the energy consistently right away. If you were already there, chances are you would not have this journal. It is also not logical to look at the list and think you have to work through and heal everything at once. Shadow Work may be an ongoing process and the behaviours and thoughts you are working on may have taken many years to develop.

To not get discouraged, and to allow you the proper time to achieve results, it is recommended that you choose one or two shadows you would like to work on before the next Full Moon. Which happens every 29.5 days. Less is more when it comes to both this and choosing your manifestations for the month. This allows you to pinpoint your energy and focus which yields quicker results.

Choose what you would like to release during this Full Moon and write it down starting with "I Release".

Make sure you are thinking about what you were manifesting during the New Moon. A huge part of this release ritual is to release anything holding you back from your manifestations.
For example: If you are manifesting financial freedom in a career you are passionate about then you may need to release bad spending habits and/or your fear of success (trust me that's more common than you think).

STEP NINE

Shadow Work Prompts

Considering the Full Moon is all about release it is a great time to work on your Shadow Work and you can do that using Shadow Work Prompts. You will find some on the next page and you can find many more on the internet. If you are new to Shadow Work, it is the process of acknowledging and healing limiting thoughts and behaviour patterns you have that may be stopping you from fully aligning with your higher self and receiving your manifestations.

It is important to note that doing Shadow Work may bring up emotions that you may not be equipped to deal with alone. Make sure you have a proper support system set up in advance to prevent feeling more discouraged than when you began. Having access to a therapist or counsellor allows you to have an unbiased opinion and proper tools for solving problems that arise. It is also good to have people you know you can trust on standby for emotional support. Just make sure you reach out to them first to make sure they have the capacity at the current time to take this on with you.

Shadow Work can be tough! So make sure you prepare a self-care activity for after each session. This not only makes you feel better but it builds positive anticipation for next time through the release of dopamine and serotonin. Try to choose activities that align with your higher self. This will not only help you during this ritual but will help you get closer to your manifestations.

If you are interested in diving deeper into shadow work make sure you check out my Guided Shadow Work Journal at http://www.kendrafierce.com.

STEP NINE - CONTINUED

The Prompts

- What are the limiting beliefs holding you back from living your dream life and how will you combat this?
- How are you? Really though??
- How do you treat people who can do nothing in return?
- If you could tell your story to someone in only a minute what would you say?
- Where do you feel like there is "not enough" in your life and how can you change your mindset around these areas?
- What are some of your looping thoughts and how can you break these cycles?
- What boundaries do you need to create with yourself to start taking better care of yourself?
- What boundaries do you need to create in your unhealthy relationships? And how will doing this make you feel?
- What situations have you given your power away and how can you reclaim this power?
- What new things would you like to learn and what's holding you back?
- What is the most empowering thing you have done and explain how it made you feel in detail?
- Who is someone you most admire and why?
- What areas of your life are you the most pessimistic about and how can you change your mindset about these areas?
- Explain something you feel guilty about and write a letter of forgiveness to yourself for the situation
- What is your personal philosophy on life?
- Write down the words you need to hear most right now
- When do you feel the most confident and why do you feel that way at that time? How can you work this feeling into more areas of your life?

STEP TEN - OPTIONAL

Burn Release

There are many reasons why people burn what they would like to release. Some people believe the act of setting something on fire brings up powerful instincts and energy. Other people believe burning them releases your intentions to your higher power. It's also thought that when you visualize the feeling of letting them go the fire solidifies them into your subconscious conscious mind. Whatever reason you choose, I can tell you from personal experience it feels pretty dang good to look your demons in the face and say "not today!" then light them on fire. Ripping them up is also an option if fire is not.

WHAT YOU'LL NEED

Small pieces of paper
Pen or pencil
Scissors or tweezers
Firesafe bowl
Water (just in case)

Step 1 | close your eyes and focus on the amazing energy you have cultivated during this ritual

Step 2 | write down what you are releasing before the next Full Moon starting with "I Release" on the small pieces of paper. You can write them all on one or one on each. Make sure they are not too big or they will be a FIRE HAZARD!

Step 3 | hold each piece of paper with the scissors or tweezers, close your eyes, and say each one out loud as you feel what it is like to release these things from your life then light them on fire or rip them up over the fire-safe bowl.

Step 4 | release the ashes under the Full Moon

STEP ELEVEN

Full Moon Bath or Shower

This Full Moon bath or shower is another mandatory activity to celebrate everything you have overcome to bring you to this moment. It is self-care to celebrate your strength and courage.

It takes a massive amount of strength to address these thoughts and situations in your life. This work may bring up a lot of uncomfortable feelings and that's okay. It is also the whole point! We do not have an unlimited capacity so releasing unwanted patterns makes room for new energy and new vibrations. Growth happens when we are uncomfortable but we also want to make sure we are balancing our work with play.

Relax and focus on rejuvenating your energy for the following two weeks. The next three phases of the moon are the waning gibbous, last quarter, and waning crescent. During this time you will want to work on your shadow work and setting healthy boundaries that align with your Higher Self. The energy of the following weeks is communication, healing, release, contemplation, and celebration.

Pamper yourself with your favourite products and never forget how absolutely INCREDIBLE you are!

The Zodiacs

As the Moon changes phases, it passes through different zodiac signs and this gives you a chance to draw upon the energy of these signs and to check into specific areas of your life.

Do these areas need a little more love and harmony?

Are there conflicts arising that relate to these areas?

As mentioned astrology is a vast subject so this journal will not be going too far in depth. However, the following is a **VERY BASIC** description of each sign and the houses they rule. To expand your understanding, please take some time and further research the aspects of the zodiacs.

Aries | March 21 – April 19
Ruling Planet | Mars
Natural Ruler | 1st House – House of Self
Aries symbolizes new beginnings and it coincides with the energy of sudden change and inspired action. Aries is energetic, independent, active, optimistic, impulsive, and open to change. An intense drive to succeed can be a double-edged sword. Ready to try new things but anxious internally due to the pressure. Upbeat, magnetic, and honest.

Taurus | April 20 – May 20
Ruling Planet | Venus
Natural Ruler | 2nd house – House of Possessions
Taurus is a fixed sign and can be very stubborn. Determined, stable, patient, practical, and affectionate. This steadfast energy perseveres with great strength. Not fond of change and has a strong need for control. Deeply sensitive, dependable, caring, and calm unless provoked.

Gemini | May 21 – June 20
Ruling Planet | Mercury
Natural Ruler | 3rd house – House of Communication
Gemini is quick in thought, energetic, versatile, and clever. Multifaceted and willing to take on any challenge. An urgent and continual need to communicate and an ongoing student of life. Persuasive, passionate, and adaptive with an uncanny zest for adventure. An intellectual with a gift for persuasion. Gifted in writing, reading, and self-expression.

Cancer | June 21 – July 22
Ruling Planet | The Moon
Natural Ruler | 4th house – House of Home
Cancer is the sign of powerful forces moving under the surface. Complicated and often misunderstood. Receptive, kind, emotional, sympathetic, and imaginative. Finding comfort in close personal relationships and support from others. A nurturer, caregiver, unpredictable, complex, and overly cautious about revealing too much. Occasionally possessive and always devoted to loved ones.

Leo | July 23 – August 22
Ruling Planet | The Sun
Natural Ruler | 5th house – House of Creativity
Exuberant and ready to take on the world! Leo is the sign of creativity, expansion, enthusiasm, hopes, wishes, and pleasure. Generally concerned more with what life has to offer them vs what they can offer the world however it's this mentality that allows Leo's to maintain their energy and unique abilities. Generous, kind, open-hearted, with larger-than-life emotions.

Virgo | August 23 – September 22
Ruling Planet | Mercury
Natural Ruler | 6th House – House of Service
Virgo is practical, industrious, intelligent, analytical, and driven. Generally, perfectionists by nature and always looking for ways to improve. Forward-thinking, intense, and adventurous. A natural over thinker with the ability to set prioritize and analyze problems logically. Always ready to put in the work to achieve whatever needs to be done even at their own sacrifice.

Libra | September 23 – October 22
Ruling Planet | Venus
Natural Ruler | 7th house – House of Partnership

Active, sociable, easygoing, charming, and diplomatic. Generally Libra is the most content functioning within partnerships and groups. Always working towards finding balance and harmony. For Libras bringing energies together feeds the soul. Magnetic and enthusiastic however somewhat indecisive. Working hard to please others and trying to control how they are viewed is a blessing and a curse.

Scorpio | October 23 – November 21
Ruling Planet | Pluto
Natural Ruler | 8th house – House of Regeneration

Passionate, persistent, unyielding, and emotional. Scorpio energy can be intense however it's this intensity that allows for success in whatever endeavor they choose. Sometimes controlling in nature however with introspection this energy can be used in powerful ways with positive results. An incredible leader, adaptable, clever, and determined with an unstoppable desire to achieve great things.

Sagittarius | November 22 – December 21
Ruling Planet | Jupiter
Natural Ruler | 9th house – House of Mental Exploration

Ambitious, generous, progressive, unconventional, and a seeker of challenges. Saggitarius is the sign of philosophy, higher learning, and broad concepts. Hard to pin down emotionally and freedom is the most prized possession. Always trying to find the silver lining in the chaos. Anything new sparks interest and the allure of adventure is what keeps this independent, unpredictable spirit alive.

Capricorn | December 22 – January 19
Ruling Planet | Saturn
Natural Ruler | 10th House – House of Career

Patient, strategic, determined, and quick to seize an opportunity. Capricorn is the sign governing reputation, career, and standing in the community. Leadership qualities are generally strong and having things in a precise, orderly fashion is important. Highly creative and also diligent. Conflicting emotions regarding responsibility and emotions requires discipline.

Aquarius | January 20 – February 18
Ruling Planet | Uranus
Natural Ruler | 11th House – House of Hopes and Humanity
Progressive, independent inventive with firm opinions. This is the sign of the visionary. Refusing to conform to the status quote and even willing to sacrifice personal relationships to maintain freedom of expression. Always asking "why" and willing to pursue goals without compromise. Content to be in social settings and just as relaxed alone. Broad-minded, honest, helpful, and never boring.

Pisces | June 21 – July 22
Ruling Planet | Neptune
Natural Ruler | 12th House – House of Secrets & Spiritual Expansion
Pisces is the last sign of the zodiac and represents the end of a cycle. Intuitive, receptive, impressionable, and adaptable. Known to have a close relationship with astral forces. Loyal, generous, and always ready to help anyone in need. Almost too giving and it's this nature that makes Pisces prone to addictions and self-undoing without intention. Compassionate, witty, imaginative, sensitive, and sentimental.

Take some time to further research not only your own birth chart but each sign in depth. Your sun sign is just a small portion of your chart so it's important to not make assumptions about not only yourself but others based on this alone.

Personalities are created and based on many factors outside of astrology. Genetics, geographical position on the planet, family structure, past trauma and so much more.

This information is best used as just a guide and as always, go with your own flow.

The Houses

As far back as Babylonian times, ancient astrologers have separated life into twelve different categories. Each house represents a category. **Fun fact,** these categories have remained almost unchanged since they came to us from that time.

Each house has a corresponding zodiac sign and each house shares qualities with that zodiac sign.

ARIES | 1st house – House of Self
TAURUS | 2nd House – House of Wealth & Possessions
GEMINI | 3rd House – House of Communication
CANCER | 4th House – House of Home
LEO | 5Th House – House of Creativity and Personal Affairs
VIRGO | 6th House – House of Health & Service
LIBRA | 7th House – House of Partnerships
SCORPIO | 8th House – House of Death & Regeneration
SAGITTARIUS | 9th House – House of Travel and Mental Exploration
CAPRICORN | 10th House – House of Career & Public Standing
AQUARIUS | 11th House – House of Dreams and Social Status
PISCES | 12 House – Secrets & Spiritual Expansion

Your birth chart is showing you where the planets were in space the day you were born. On your birth chart, any house with one or more planets is strengthened by the energy of that planet. Each planet will be in a specific zodiac sign in a specific house.

During the New and Full Moon you can check to see what sign they are in and check your birth chart to see where those signs are in your birth chart and what houses they are in. If you are experiencing heavy emotions you can check into these areas to see if they need a little extra TLC. If you don't see those specific zodiac signs, during the moons you can go by the signs natural house ruler as they are listed above.

The Journal

No matter what happens we can always count on the Moon changing phases. Astronomy and astrology are complex subjects and have been a part of humanity for thousands of years and there is a lot of information available. My hope is with the **Moon Phases Guided Journal** you are able to build a stronger foundation not only spiritually but scientifically using the phases of the Moon as a guide.

Putting inspired action to your inspired ideas will help you change your vibration to align with that of your Higher Self and manifestations. Taking time twice a month to complete these rituals, connect with your Higher Self, create goals, and work on releasing what no longer serves you will not only keep you on a consistent schedule but you will find your manifestations appearing quicker than you ever thought possible.

Your thoughts align your emotions which aligns your actions and that's manifestation. Every thing else is just a tool to help you get on the level of your manifestations. **My biggest recommendation is to always go with your own flow and try not restrict yourself too much with "rules" about how and when things should be done.**

Remember the Moon is only full for less than and minute and the phases are constantly changing. You are not missing anything and you are exactly where you need to be when you need to be there.

The rest of the **Moon Phases Guided Journal** is filled with blank, guided pages that coincide with the New and Full Moon Rituals described.

Phases

| Aries | Taurus | Gemini | Cancer | Leo | Virgo | Libra | Scorpio | Sagittarius | Capricorn | Aquarius | Pisces |

Date: _____ Zodiac: _____

I currently feel: _____
_____
_____
_____
_____
_____
_____
_____
_____
_____
_____

The energy I am bringing into this session is: _____
_____
_____

I am grateful for: _____
_____
_____
_____
_____

_____
_____
_____
_____
_____

My higher self is:

_____   _____
_____   _____
_____   _____
_____   _____

Limiting thoughts & behaviour patterns I am working on (shadows):

_____
_____
_____
_____
_____
_____
_____
_____
_____
_____
_____
_____
_____
_____

Letter of manifestation or letter of forgiveness:

I RELEASE ANY AND ALL ENERGY ATTACHED TO THESE SITUATIONS FOR MY OWN PERSONAL GROWTH AND HEALING.
SIGNED:

Prompts/Notes for next time

Phases

Aries Taurus Gemini Cancer Leo Virgo Libra Scorpio Sagittarius Capricorn Aquarius Pisces

Date: _____ Zodiac: _____

I currently feel: _____
_____
_____
_____
_____
_____
_____
_____
_____
_____
_____
_____

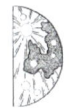

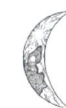

The energy I am bringing into this session is: _____
_____
_____

I am grateful for: _____
_____
_____
_____
_____

___

___

___

___

My higher self is:

___

___

___

___

Limiting thoughts & behaviour patterns I am working on (shadows):

___

___

___

___

___

___

___

___

___

___

___

___

Letter of manifestation or letter of forgiveness:

I RELEASE ANY AND ALL ENERGY ATTACHED TO THESE SITUATIONS FOR MY OWN PERSONAL GROWTH AND HEALING.
SIGNED:

Prompts/Notes for next time

Phases

| Aries | Taurus | Gemini | Cancer | Leo | Virgo | Libra | Scorpio | Sagittarius | Capricorn | Aquarius | Pisces |

Date: _____ Zodiac: _____

I currently feel: _____
_____
_____
_____
_____
_____
_____
_____
_____
_____
_____
_____

The energy I am bringing into this session is: _____
_____
_____

I am grateful for: _____
_____
_____
_____
_____

My higher self is:

Limiting thoughts & behaviour patterns I am working on (shadows):

Letter of manifestation or letter of forgiveness:

I RELEASE ANY AND ALL ENERGY ATTACHED TO THESE SITUATIONS FOR MY OWN PERSONAL GROWTH AND HEALING.
SIGNED:

Prompts/Notes for next time

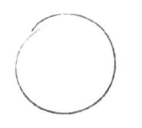

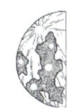

Phases

| Aries | Taurus | Gemini | Cancer | Leo | Virgo | Libra | Scorpio | Sagittarius | Capricorn | Aquarius | Pisces |

Date: _____ Zodiac: _____

I currently feel: _____

_____
_____
_____
_____
_____
_____
_____
_____
_____
_____
_____

The energy I am bringing into this session is: _____

_____
_____

I am grateful for: _____

_____
_____
_____
_____

My higher self is:

Limiting thoughts & behaviour patterns I am working on (shadows):

Letter of manifestation or letter of forgiveness:

I RELEASE ANY AND ALL ENERGY ATTACHED TO THESE SITUATIONS FOR MY OWN PERSONAL GROWTH AND HEALING.

SIGNED:

Prompts/Notes for next time

Phases

| Aries | Taurus | Gemini | Cancer | Leo | Virgo | Libra | Scorpio | Sagittarius | Capricorn | Aquarius | Pisces |

Date: _____ Zodiac: _____

I currently feel: _____
_____
_____
_____
_____
_____
_____
_____
_____
_____
_____
_____

The energy I am bringing into this session is: _____
_____
_____

I am grateful for: _____
_____
_____
_____
_____
_____

My higher self is:

Limiting thoughts & behaviour patterns I am working on (shadows):

Letter of manifestation or letter of forgiveness:

I RELEASE ANY AND ALL ENERGY ATTACHED TO THESE SITUATIONS FOR MY OWN PERSONAL GROWTH AND HEALING.
SIGNED:

Prompts/Notes for next time

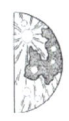

Phases

| Aries | Taurus | Gemini | Cancer | Leo | Virgo | Libra | Scorpio | Sagittarius | Capricorn | Aquarius | Pisces |

Date: _____ Zodiac: _____

I currently feel: _____

_____

_____

_____

_____

_____

_____

_____

_____

_____

_____

The energy I am bringing into this session is: _____

_____

_____

I am grateful for: _____

_____

_____

_____

_____

My higher self is:

Limiting thoughts & behaviour patterns I am working on (shadows):

Letter of manifestation or letter of forgiveness:

_____
_____
_____
_____
_____
_____
_____
_____
_____
_____
_____
_____
_____
_____
_____
_____
_____
_____
_____
_____
_____
_____
_____
_____
_____

I RELEASE ANY AND ALL ENERGY ATTACHED TO THESE SITUATIONS FOR MY OWN PERSONAL GROWTH AND HEALING.

SIGNED: _____

Prompts/Notes for next time

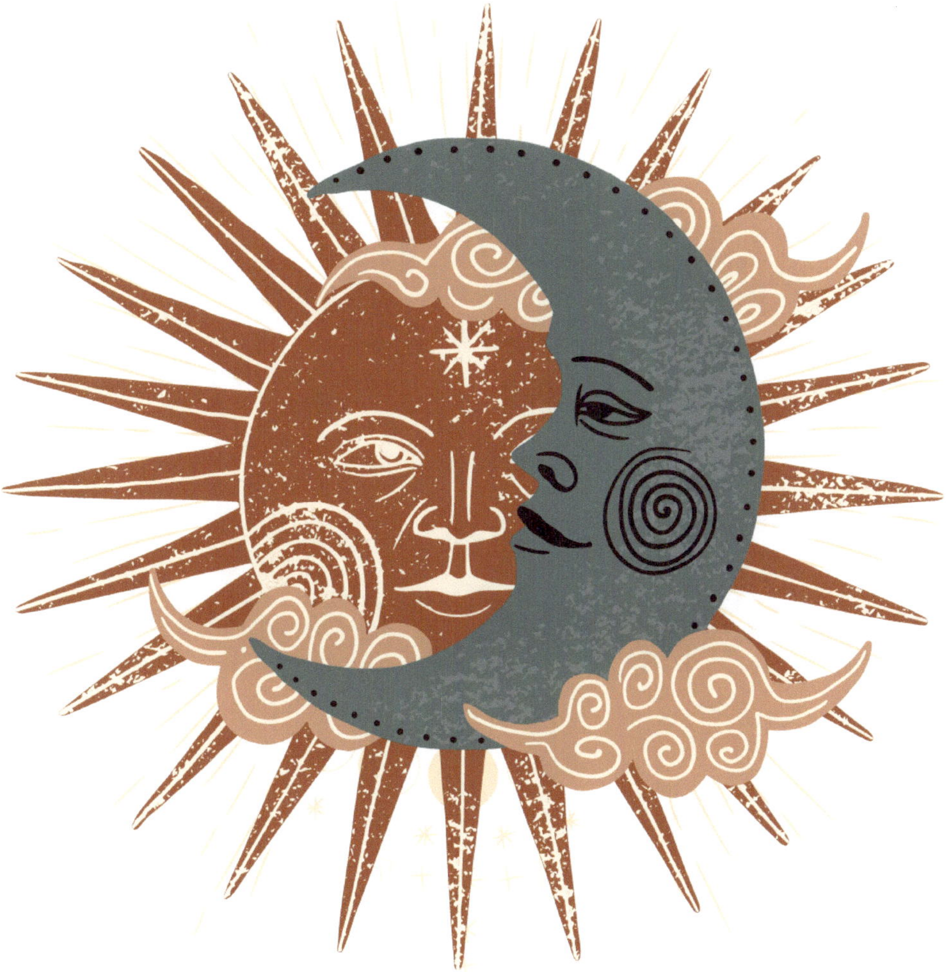

Manufactured by Amazon.ca
Bolton, ON